ABUNDANT TRUTH INTERNATIONAL MINISTRIES

Abundant Truth Spiritual Gifts Series

INTERPRETING DREAMS AND VISIONS

A Biblical Approach to Interpreting Dreams and Visions

Roderick Levi Evans

Published by Abundant Truth Publishing
P.O. Box 126
Camden, NC 27921
Web: www.abundantpublishing.net
Email: abundantpublishing@gmail.com

Printed U.S.A.

Front & Back Cover Designs by Abundant Truth Publishing
All rights reserved.
Free-use Cover Image

Abundant Truth Publishing is a ministry of **Abundant Truth International Ministries.** The primary mission of ATI Ministries is to equip the Body of Christ with tools necessary to defend and contend for the truth of the Christian faith. Jesus Christ came to bear witness of the truth and ATI Ministries is a modern-day extension of His commission (John 18:37).

Abundant Truth Spiritual Gifts Series– Interpreting Dreams and Visions
©2022 Abundant Truth Publishing
All Rights Reserved
ISBN13: 978-1601411921

Printed in the United States of America

Unless otherwise indicated, all of the scripture quotations are taken from the *Authorized King James Version* of the Bible. Scripture quotations marked with NIV are taken from the *New International Version* of the Bible. Scripture quotations marked with NASV are taken from the *New American Standard Version* of the Bible. Scripture quotations marked with Amplified are taken from the *Amplified Bi*

Contents

Introduction

Chapter 1 – Understanding Biblical Symbols   1

Animals   *4*

Sun, Moon, Stars, and Planets   *9*

Landscape, Fields, and Mountains   *12*

Water, Oil, and Wine   *14*

Events and Acts of Nature   *16*

Numbers   *17*

Chapter 2 – Understanding Personal & Cultural Symbols   23

Past Events/Things/Objects   *25*

Contents (cont.)

People and Places	*26*
Cultural Stories and Education	*28*
Death and/or Funeral	*30*
Sexual Activity or Intimacy	*32*

Chapter 3 – Interpreting Dreams and Visions — **39**

Know Your Bible	*45*
Know Your God	*47*
Know Yourself	*50*

Chapter 4 – Now Concerning Dreams and Visions — **57**

How to Apply Dreams and Visions	*59*

Contents (cont.)

Final Thoughts on Dreams and Visions   65

Introduction

The promise of the Father was the fulfillment of God's prophecy through Joel. One result of the Spirit's coming would be prophetic revelation and the manifestation of dreams and visions. We discover from Paul's discussions of the gifts in I Corinthian 12 that the Spirit is responsible for the dispersion of the gifts. In the Abundant Truth Spiritual Gifts Series, we will examine the gifts of the Spirit and their operations in the New Testament Church.

In this publication:

This publication presents a solid foundation for interpreting dreams and visions. When Jesus made us citizens of the Kingdom, it came with advantages. As members of the kingdom of God, we are eligible to partake of the outpouring of the Spirit.

The books of Joel and the Acts declare that the direct result of the outpouring of the Spirit of God would be revelation. Men and women could receive and communicate by the Spirit of God; two ways this is done is through ***dreams and***

visions.

And it shall come to pass afterward, that I will pour out my spirit upon all flesh; and your sons and your daughters shall prophesy, your old men shall dream dreams, your young men shall see visions. (Joel 2:28)

But this is that which was spoken by the prophet Joel; And it shall come to pass in the last days, saith God, I will pour out of my Spirit upon all flesh: and your sons and your daughters shall prophesy, and your young men shall see visions, and your old men shall dream dreams. (Acts 2:16, 17)

In the first book of this two-part series, we presented a proper foundation for the place of dreams and visions in the lives of His servants. Now, we will discuss the interpretation of dreams and visions. We will examine the different symbols of dreams and visions, and how to apply them in the Christian life.

INTERPRETING DREAMS AND VISIONS

- Chapter 1 -
Understanding Biblical Symbols

INTERPRETING DREAMS AND VISIONS

INTERPRETING DREAMS AND VISIONS

The scriptures are an excellent source in discovering the meaning of a dream or vision. God has a language of His own. He uses His creation to show forth His glory.

This is an important fact in understanding symbols He uses. Both Testaments show consistency in symbols that God uses to express His plan and purposes.

Now, there are too many to discuss, but we will look at 6 common symbols used by God in dreams and visions.

INTERPRETING DREAMS AND VISIONS

The heavens declare the glory of God; and the firmament sheweth his handywork. Psalms 19:1 (KJV)

Animals

In the scriptures, God repeatedly used animals as symbols in dreams and visions. When this was done, it was to describe the nature and character of a person.

In the book of Daniel, we discover that when God wanted to talk about the nations, He gave Daniel visions of various animals and creatures to describe the

INTERPRETING DREAMS AND VISIONS

activities of the nations and their leaders.

> *Daniel spake and said, I saw in my vision by night, and, behold, the four winds of the heaven strove upon the great sea. And four great beasts came up from the sea, diverse one from another. Dan 7:2-3 (KJV)*

When you see animals in dreams, it will be usually in references to individuals that are around you or that you will encounter. God will show the animal rather than the individual at times so that you will see them properly without any external

INTERPRETING DREAMS AND VISIONS

barriers.

God's use of animals in dreams and visions is not to be seen always as a negative thing. The nature of Christ was revealed in animal symbolism. John the Baptist referred to Him as the lamb of God.

The next day John seeth Jesus coming unto him, and saith, Behold the Lamb of God, which taketh away the sin of the world. John 1:29 (KJV)

To describe the different nations and kindreds of people that would enter into the kingdom of God, Jesus used fish as a

INTERPRETING DREAMS AND VISIONS

symbol.

> *Again, the kingdom of heaven is like unto a net, that was cast into the sea, and gathered of every kind: Which, when it was full, they drew to shore, and sat down, and gathered the good into vessels, but cast the bad away.* Matt 13:47-48 (KJV)

Conversely, the ungodly Pharisees and false prophets are referred to as vipers and wolves, respectively.

> *But when he saw many of the Pharisees and Sadducees come to his*

INTERPRETING DREAMS AND VISIONS

baptism, he said unto them, O generation of vipers, who hath warned you to flee from the wrath to come? Matt 3:7 (KJV)

Beware of false prophets, which come to you in sheep's clothing, but inwardly they are ravening wolves. Matt 7:15 (KJV)

Therefore, animals in dreams usually represent people and their characters.

Always remember that the inspiration of the Holy Spirit will give you the proper application.

INTERPRETING DREAMS AND VISIONS

Sun, Moon, Stars, and Planets

God used the celestial bodies to represent those in authority and leaders. Remember, in Joseph's dreams, his parents were represented by the sun and moon and his brothers were represented by the stars.

> *Behold, I have dreamed a dream more; and, behold, the sun and the moon and the eleven stars made obeisance to me. (Genesis 37:9)*

Joseph was the youngest (aside from Benjamin) of his brothers. In Hebraic culture, he was considered inferior and

INTERPRETING DREAMS AND VISIONS

under their authority. Therefore, in his dream, God conveyed that those in authority over him would bow to him. Other times in the scriptures, stars were used to describe angels.

> *When the morning stars sang together, and all the sons of God shouted for joy? Job 38:7 (KJV)*

Again, we see authority and power connected to heavenly bodies. In the Book of Revelation, Jesus was seen in the vision holding seven stars in His hands.

The mystery of the seven stars

INTERPRETING DREAMS AND VISIONS

which thou sawest in my right hand, and the seven golden candlesticks. The seven stars are the angels of the seven churches: and the seven candlesticks which thou sawest are the seven churches. Rev 1:20 (KJV)

Jesus stated that the stars were the angels (not divine beings), but the pastors/leaders of the churches. Here we see that stars are reflecting those in authority. Hence, when we see the sun, moon, stars, and planets, they usually are referring to those in authority, including God and Christ.

INTERPRETING DREAMS AND VISIONS

Landscapes, Fields, and Mountains

God used fields and landscapes to describe multitudes of people. In addition, they were used to describe one's labor and journey. You may see hills and valleys which describe the joys and ills of life as well as the different things that one has to endure.

And thou saidst, I will surely do thee good, and make thy seed as the sand of the sea, which cannot be numbered for multitude. Gen 32:12 (KJV)

He told Abraham that his seed would

INTERPRETING DREAMS AND VISIONS

be as the sand of the sea. Even in his parable of the wheat and the tares, Jesus described the man's field as the world. Even when talking about the task of winning souls, Jesus said that the fields were white.

> *Say not ye, There are yet four months, and then cometh harvest? behold, I say unto you, Lift up your eyes, and look on the fields; for they are white already to harvest. John 4:35 (KJV)*

When you see landscapes and terrains, God usually is showing you

INTERPRETING DREAMS AND VISIONS

something concerning your work and labor in Him, as well as speaking to you of people who are involved in that labor.

Water, Oil, Wine

Repeatedly, God used oil, wine, and water as a symbol of His presence; that is, the Holy Spirit. In the book of Ezekiel, the glory of God was seen as a river of water.

> *Afterward he brought me again unto the door of the house; and, behold, waters issued out from under the threshold of the house eastward: for the forefront of the house stood*

INTERPRETING DREAMS AND VISIONS

toward the east, and the waters came down from under from the right side of the house, at the south side of the altar. Ezek 47:1 (KJV)

Jesus, when speaking of the Spirit abiding in an individual referred to it as living water.

He that believeth on me, as the scripture hath said, out of his belly shall flow rivers of living water. (But this spake he of the Spirit, which they that believe on him should receive: John 7:38-39 (KJV)

INTERPRETING DREAMS AND VISIONS

Depending upon the dream and/or vision and its context, water will represent a move of God or a spiritual renewing. It sometimes will be seen as new life.

Events and Acts of Nature

God uses acts of nature; that is, storms, fires, sunrises, sunsets, and the like to convey His message in dreams and visions. Depending upon the dream, storms usually reveal hard times that will be in your life while peaceful scenes represent refreshing, newness, and the peace of God.

INTERPRETING DREAMS AND VISIONS

Usually, God will use the backdrop of nature in a dream to reveal to you times and seasons in your life or in the life of another.

Numbers

It would take too long to discuss the many uses of numbers in dreams and visions. The biblical record abounds with God's use of numbers to convey His message. Numbers could point to various things.

Jesus was in the grave three days and three nights. If you see 3, it could represent

INTERPRETING DREAMS AND VISIONS

a time of transition and purpose.

> *For as Jonas was three days and three nights in the whale's belly; so shall the Son of man be three days and three nights in the heart of the earth. Matt 12:40 (KJV)*

The number seven could represent completion or fullness because God created the earth in seven days and then rested.

> *And on the seventh day God ended his work which he had made; and he rested on the seventh day from all his*

INTERPRETING DREAMS AND VISIONS

work which he had made. Gen 2:2 (KJV)

The number ten may represent testing and trials. Jesus told the Church in Revelation that they would be tested, having tribulation for 10 days.

Fear none of those things which thou shalt suffer: behold, the devil shall cast some of you into prison, that ye may be tried; and ye shall have tribulation ten days: be thou faithful unto death, and I will give thee a crown of life. Rev 2:10 (KJV)

INTERPRETING DREAMS AND VISIONS

So, we see that numbers can point to different things. Prayer and careful discernment will be needed when you see or hear numbers in dreams. But, God does use them frequently and with a specific purpose in mind.

INTERPRETING DREAMS AND VISIONS

Notes:

INTERPRETING DREAMS AND VISIONS

-Chapter 2-
Understanding Personal &Cultural Symbols

INTERPRETING DREAMS AND VISIONS

INTERPRETING DREAMS AND VISIONS

God will not only use biblical symbols when speaking to us in dreams and visions but will also use things that are common and familiar to us. He knows everything about us and the things that have impacted us. Hence, things will show up in dreams and visions that we hold the key to understanding them. We will look at 5 common categories.

Past Events/Things/Objects

If you have experiences, bad and good, that have impacted you greatly, these may show up in dreams and visions.

INTERPRETING DREAMS AND VISIONS

For instance, if there is a song that you associate with joy or sadness, you may have a dream or vision in which you hear that song.

Whatever you associate it with is what God is incorporating into what you are being shown. So, if the song reminds you of joy, God could be showing you that you are entering into a time of peace and joy in Him, etc.

People and Places

You may have dreams and visions involving people and places you have not

INTERPRETING DREAMS AND VISIONS

seen in years. God uses these to point to different parts of you. Whatever you associate the person or place with, is what God is saying to you at that time.

If you see people who are mean-spirited, God could be showing you some aggressive parts of your nature. If you see people who were push-overs, He could be showing you that you need to take a stand.

For instance, years ago, I had a dream that I was back at a place where I was formerly employed. Now, the dream was

INTERPRETING DREAMS AND VISIONS

not intended to tell me to go back to work for this company, but God was showing me that I had returned to some old ways and activities. He used something that was common to me to point to something that was happening internally.

Cultural Stories and Education

God also will use cultural symbols and things that we have learned during the course of our education to reveal things to us. You may have dreams which remind you of nursery rhymes or historical events.

INTERPRETING DREAMS AND VISIONS

Whatever these things meant to you will give insight as to the meaning and interpretation of your dream or vision.

Wherein were all manner of fourfooted beasts of the earth, and wild beasts, and creeping things, and fowls of the air. And there came a voice to him, Rise, Peter; kill, and eat. But Peter said, Not so, Lord; for I have never eaten anything that is common or unclean. And the voice spake unto him again the second time, What God hath cleansed, that call not thou common. Acts 10:12-15 (KJV)

INTERPRETING DREAMS AND VISIONS

When God spoke to Peter (in a trance) about the Gentiles and the faith, He used the Jewish dietary restrictions to convey His message.

Death and/or Funeral

Except the dream is a literal dream, when one sees death, God is symbolizing a person's need to "die" to something so that He can bring them into something new.

Many become afraid when they see death believing that something bad is going to happen, when actually the Lord is

INTERPRETING DREAMS AND VISIONS

calling them to give up or turn away from certain things. It could also mean spiritual death.

Ezekiel had a vision of dead, dry bones signifying the physical and spiritual demise of Israel as a nation.

The hand of the Lord was upon me, and carried me out in the spirit of the Lord, and set me down in the midst of the valley which was full of bones. Ezek 37:1 (KJV)

Hence, scenes of death may refer to spiritual decline or loss. If the dream is

INTERPRETING DREAMS AND VISIONS

concerning someone else, it may be the Lord revealing to you an area in their life that needs to be dealt with. Also, it could speak of spiritual death.

God may be revealing that you or an individual have lost some zeal and fervor for life in Christ. This is why Jesus said to John that the people had a name that they were alive but were dead in the book of Revelation.

Sexual Activity or Intimacy

First, understand that God is holy and will not tempt us with sin in a dream.

INTERPRETING DREAMS AND VISIONS

When we speak of sexual activity or intimacy in a dream or vision, it will be "G-rated." God will show you things to convey His point without stirring up the wrong types of feelings.

When God gives dreams of this nature, it is usually in reference to a person's connection with someone else. We know that God would refer to Israel's actions with other nations as adulterous, as an act of prostitution, and as an affair.

They say, If a man put away his wife, and she go from him, and become

INTERPRETING DREAMS AND VISIONS

another man's, shall he return unto her again? shall not that land be greatly polluted? but thou hast played the harlot with many lovers; yet return again to me, saith the Lord. Jer 3:1 (KJV)

These are sexual terms, but He was describing their connection and involvement. These types of dreams will show you, most of the time, unfruitful connections in your life and others, which have nothing at all to do with actual sexual activity.

Seeing partial nakedness is a dream

INTERPRETING DREAMS AND VISIONS

usually means that God is uncovering hidden things in someone's life or it could be a call to humility.

> *Because thou sayest, I am rich, and increased with goods, and have need of nothing; and knowest not that thou art wretched, and miserable, and poor, and blind, and naked. Rev 3:17 (KJV)*

Jesus said that the Laodiceans were poor, blind, and naked. Nakedness was a reference to their spiritual lack and necessary. It will convey the same message

INTERPRETING DREAMS AND VISIONS

in dreams and visions.

Even though we have enumerated some of the symbols that appear in dreams and visions, remember nothing is "set in stone" and God will use what He wants, how He wants to convey His message. With this in mind, let us look at keys to interpreting dreams and visions.

Question for Personal Reflection: What Symbols Biblical, Personal, or Cultural do you regularly see in your dreams or visions?

INTERPRETING DREAMS AND VISIONS

Notes:

INTERPRETING DREAMS AND VISIONS

-Chapter 3-
Interpreting Dreams and Visions

INTERPRETING DREAMS AND VISIONS

INTERPRETING DREAMS AND VISIONS

Throughout the ages, discovering the interpretations of dreams and visions have troubled many and excited others. We have discussed the types of dreams and visions and reasons for their occurrence.

Now, we will discuss the actual interpretation of dreams and visions. As we discuss dream/vision interpretation, keep one truth in mind:

All Interpretations Come From God

Though we will offer some guides and clues to dream interpretation, we must remember that if God sends or gives a

INTERPRETING DREAMS AND VISIONS

dream or vision, He has a particular purpose in mind.

Hence, your confidence to find interpretation will not rest upon your ability or intellect, but upon God who is able to reveal all things. We make this initial statement of truth from the biblical account of Joseph in Egypt.

While in the Egyptian prison and before Pharaoh, he made the following two declarations.

And Joseph said unto them, Do not interpretations belong to God? tell

INTERPRETING DREAMS AND VISIONS

me them, I pray you. Gen 40:8 (KJV)

And Joseph answered Pharaoh, saying, It is not in me: God shall give Pharaoh an answer of peace. Gen 41:16 (KJV)

When you approach the interpretation of dreams and visions understand that:

It is not in you, but in God – you can trust that He will give proper understanding.

The interpretation rests with God – He knows the reason and purpose behind the dream or vision.

INTERPRETING DREAMS AND VISIONS

These two facts should provoke a sense of peace in those who are faced with discovering interpretations. We also know that sometimes God will preserve the interpretation of a dream or vision to be shared by someone other than ourselves.

This is to promote unity and interdependence in the body of Christ.

We began this chapter by stating that interpretation belongs to God. The burden of interpretation does not rest upon us, but God. However, there are

INTERPRETING DREAMS AND VISIONS

things we must know to be in a proper place to receive the correct interpretation.

Know Your Bible

We have already stated that the scriptures are an excellent source for dream and vision interpretation. The Bible is full of stories of God's communication, interaction, and involvement with man. Jesus stated we should live by His word.

> *But he answered and said, It is written, Man shall not live by bread alone, but by every word that proceedeth out of the mouth of God. Matt 4:4 (KJV)*

INTERPRETING DREAMS AND VISIONS

The scriptures help you to understand how God speaks and what He uses to convey His message to His people. David, in the Psalms, stated that the word was a lamp and light.

> *Thy word is a lamp unto my feet, and a light unto my path. Psalms 119:105 KJV*

The Scriptures will bring illumination to the symbols and their meanings shown in dreams and visions. Scriptures provide a definite framework for symbols and their interpretation. When you rely on the

INTERPRETING DREAMS AND VISIONS

Scriptures for assistance in interpretation, you can better discern.

Paul told Timothy that all scripture is profitable, this even applies to dream interpretation.

Know Your God

When we say, "know your God," we are referring to you knowing His voice and the inspiration of the Holy Spirit. In order for you to understand properly the interpretation of a dream or vision, you have to know the voice of Christ through the Holy Spirit.

INTERPRETING DREAMS AND VISIONS

My sheep hear my voice, and I know them, and they follow me: John 10:27 (KJV)

Since God will use many symbols and events to convey His message, you have to be sensitive to Him so that you can receive from Him.

When you know His voice, even if He uses someone else to interpret your dream or vision, you will be able to receive it.

Also, you must know the nature of God. When you understand His nature, you

INTERPRETING DREAMS AND VISIONS

will be able to understand what is seen through His eyes. Dreams from the Lord will not only reveal His purpose, but His character.

> *But let him that glorieth glory in this, that he understandeth and knoweth me, that I am the Lord which exercise lovingkindness, judgment, and righteousness, in the earth: for in these things I delight, saith the Lord. Jer 9:24 (KJV)*

God is governed by holiness, righteousness, and love. Your dreams

INTERPRETING DREAMS AND VISIONS

should reveal this about God as you endeavor to interpret them.

Dreams will never come to break up marriages, bring discord in the Church, reveal others' weaknesses without giving a remedy for them, or inspire ungodly anger in you.

Know Yourself

Since every dream does not come from the inspiration of God, you have to be able to recognize when a dream is coming because of you; that is, events and concerns in your life.

INTERPRETING DREAMS AND VISIONS

In this way, you will not spend unnecessary time trying to interpret a dream that did not come from God. It will also help you to recognize when a dream and vision is of God; that you can give it proper prayer and consideration.

> *Behold, thou desirest truth in the nward parts: and in the hidden part thou shalt make me to know wisdom. Psalms 51:6 (KJV)*

Since men are vulnerable to error, self-awareness is a vital part to discerning the source, especially of dreams. You must

INTERPRETING DREAMS AND VISIONS

know what tempts you.

You must know your personal desires, temptations, and ambitions. These could show up in dreams and be received as revelation from the Lord when it is only your desires.

In addition, you must know what scares you. Fears can show up in dreams. Some, then, mistake them to be warnings. Yet, they are only manifestations of personal concerns.

Prayer is also important in interpreting dreams and visions. And never forget, the

INTERPRETING DREAMS AND VISIONS

input of others could prove to be most helpful. God still uses dreams and visions to speak to His people. They are not given to frustrate us, but to encourage us and take us further in our relationship with Christ.

INTERPRETING DREAMS AND VISIONS

INTERPRETING DREAMS AND VISIONS

Notes:

INTERPRETING DREAMS AND VISIONS

INTERPRETING DREAMS AND VISIONS

-Chapter 4-
Now Concerning Dreams and Visions

INTERPRETING DREAMS AND VISIONS

INTERPRETING DREAMS AND VISIONS

We wanted to conclude our discussion by listing other facets concerning dreams and visions that may not have been discussed earlier.

These are given to help clarify certain points as we endeavor to hear God speak to us through dreams and visions.

How to Apply Dreams and Visions

To minimize confusion that comes from dream and vision interpretation, there are guidelines that believers can incorporate after having a dream or vision. These will help in interpreting and applying

INTERPRETING DREAMS AND VISIONS

dreams and visions.

1. Be prayerful about the dream or vision.

After having a dream or vision, pray throughout the day for clarity and understanding. This will help in recognizing the interpretation and source.

Pray without ceasing. (I Thessalonians 5:17)

2. Meditate upon symbols and scenarios.

Though dreams and visions come with plot lines and images, some parts in

INTERPRETING DREAMS AND VISIONS

them are for impact and may not be the focal point or purpose. Hence, meditating upon what was seen will help to center one's attention on what the Lord was conveying or saying.

Give ye ear, and hear my voice; hearken, and hear my speech. (Isaiah 28:23)

3. Receive dreams and visions in a humble manner.

There are times when dreams and visions will show you great blessings and ministries. Sometimes, God will reveal

INTERPRETING DREAMS AND VISIONS

secret things. You must remain humble in order to receive what was shown and apply it properly.

> *Likewise, ye younger, submit yourselves unto the elder. Yea, all of you be subject one to another, and be clothed with humility: for God resisteth the proud, And giveth grace to the humble. (I Peter 5:5)*

4. Discuss the dream and vision with mature believers.

Certain believers (leaders and prayer partners) may be able to help you

INTERPRETING DREAMS AND VISIONS

understand other aspects of the dream and/or vision.

Sometimes we receive dreams and visions in self-centered terms. Other eyes may be able to see more clearly what the Lord is referring to with particular dreams and visions.

Where no counsel is, the people fall: but in the multitude of counselors there is safety. (Proverbs 11:14)

5. Fulfill all known requirements for the dream and/or vision's fulfillment.

Certain dreams and visions come with

INTERPRETING DREAMS AND VISIONS

conditions of fulfillment. While you are waiting for God to do His work, do your part. In addition, some dreams and visions may not specifically outline conditions, but the conditions may be implied.

> *If you fully obey the LORD your God and carefully follow all his commands I give you today, the LORD your God will set you high above all the nations on earth. (Deuteronomy 28:1)*

6. Walk in faith until you see its fulfillment.

The enemy will come to try to strip the

INTERPRETING DREAMS AND VISIONS

believer of faith in the dream or vision. Therefore, fight the deception of the enemy with faith and the revelation of the dream and/or vision.

That ye be not slothful, but followers of them who through faith and patience inherit the promises. (Hebrews 6:12)

Final Thoughts on Dreams and Visions

- ➢ God will use others to interpret your dreams.
- ➢ Symbols common to you will be used most often in dreams and visions.

INTERPRETING DREAMS AND VISIONS

- Visions normally reveal things in God's eternal purpose in the lives of people.
- Much prayer and discernment is needed in discovering interpretations.
- The interpretation of a dream and/or vision ultimately rests upon the revelation of God.
- Having a dream within a dream usually means that it is established. The thing shown will happen.
- Reoccurring dreams and visions usually come when one has not followed their

INTERPRETING DREAMS AND VISIONS

instructions.

➢ If you dream regularly, start a dream journal to help with memory and interpretation.

INTERPRETING DREAMS AND VISIONS

INTERPRETING DREAMS AND VISIONS

Notes:

_____

_____

_____

_____

_____

_____

_____

_____

_____

_____

INTERPRETING DREAMS AND VISIONS

www.ingramcontent.com/pod-product-compliance
Lightning Source LLC
Chambersburg PA
CBHW050343010526
44119CB00049B/677